MW00710340

Your Journal Companion:
365 Writing Prompts

to
Heighten Awareness
of
Self and Others

by
Plynn Gutman

Printed by CreateSpace, an Amazon.com company

Book Design: Edith Jennison
Author's Photo: Mitchell Gutman

Self Help Techniques; Writing Techniques; Mind-Body; Spirituality

ISBN: 978-0-9904646-1-7

Published by:
Plynn Gutman & PLG Press
Mesa, Arizona, USA

Dedication:

To our Higher Self,
the keeper of knowledge that can transform us,
if we but give it a forum to speak.

Table of Contents

Acknowledgements

Many people have contributed to the writing of this book, as it comes from a rich compilation of teachers I've had, books I've read, students I've taught, and the pages and pages of experiences I've shared in my personal journals. All have spoken into my life, supported my dreams and aspirations (directly or indirectly), and infused me with the kind of love that supports "creation."

First, a big thank you to my coaching colleague Patti Oskvarek, for saying, after attending one of my journaling workshops, "You should write a book on this!" and then gently holding me accountable to do it. To my mentor and friend, G. Lynn Nelson, thank you for teaching me to write from the heart and for giving me the opportunity to work with the wonderful, young writers of YAWP for six years. These experiences are infused in the pages of Your Journal Companion. Many thanks to Lorie Warnock for your care-full reading of the manuscript, and Edith Jennison for the beautiful book cover, expertly done formatting and your marketing tutelage. Thanks to Lisa and Rex Bell for providing your delightful Laguna cottage as my "Creation Station" for this book and to the Pacific Ocean for nurturing my creative flow. And finally, my deepest thanks go to my faithful and loving family ~ Michael, Mitchell and Daniel ~ for always, always being there for me, no matter what wild and crazy adventure I choose to embark upon. No one could be more blessed.

Introduction

I offer this journal companion from the heart of my own experience with the journaling process, which I have been using, almost daily, for the past twenty-five years. My journal has been the place where I speak my truth, pour out my heart, mull over problems, plan and dream, stir my creativity and chronicle the days of my life.

It has listened – without judgment – to my concerns about health issues, family difficulties and the big questions about the meaning of my life. Too, it care-fully holds my poems, snippets of stories, details of vivid dreams, words of wisdom from my Higher Self and from others – the tender beginnings of change and inspiration.

My journal is what I want it to be, what I need it to be, each time I open it and put my pen to the page. This is what a journal is meant to be.

In general, I have discovered that there is a misconception about journaling. I've often heard people say, "Oh no, if using a journal means writing, I can't do that." Followed by, "I'm not a writer" or "I don't like writing" or most frequently, "I'm not good at writing." A blanket statement and likely a raw remnant of a mindset put upon them by some well-meaning (or not so well-meaning) teacher, who red-marked their school writing and liberally issued C's and D's.

Journal writing is not school writing, which is meant to be critiqued for the purposes of improving skills. Instead, it is the freely written expression of one's heart, soul, mind and emotions, never to be read by another human being unless the journaler chooses to share. There are no red pen corrections, no spelling or grammar checkers, no content police, no performance judges – just you, your thoughts and doodles, and your journal.

And, here's the next thing I hear people say, "Okay, so I reveal my inner most thoughts and feelings in my journal. What if someone reads it without my permission?"

This is a particularly potent issue for children and teens, whose privacy is often still at the discretion of parents. And it is a genuine concern for anyone who desires privacy.

The first step to maintaining privacy is to keep what you are doing to yourself. It is no one's business to know that you are keeping a journal. In my experience, the best results of this process are accomplished when you are alone and quiet with your own thoughts. Or, if you choose to write in a public place, you are anonymous so, essentially, no one cares.

Unless you keep your journal with you at all times – and I know many people who do – then it is important to find a secure place to store it from the prying eyes of family and friends. The human species is curious, so even with those you trust, you are inviting invasion. Therefore, please, don't leave your journal unattended on the coffee table or your nightstand.

If others are aware of your journal keeping, then a heartfelt conversation about respecting your privacy may be in order. I have discovered that the less said, the better. The less attention you bring to your journal with regard to others, the less interest they will have in spying on you.

My final advice on this issue is that if, by chance, someone does read your journal then maybe, in the universal scheme of things, that person was meant to read it, and that the revelation of your words ultimately impacts both you and the person for good.

From Saint Paul and Francis of Assisi, to Abraham Lincoln and Benjamin Franklin, to artists such as Sonya Tolstoy, Virginia Wolff and Ray Bradbury, people from all walks of life have been using the journaling process for centuries. "Journal" is only the contemporary word for "diary." Though many of us equate a diary with chronicling events – and we know that much historical information has been gleaned from the writings of important religious, social and political figures – threaded amidst the dates and events are also private thoughts, concerns and ruminations. These are the words that give us a sense of community with the universal human condition as well as the assurance that we all feel, we all have fears, we all have the need to express the concerns of our heart.

The writer, E. M. Forster said, "How can I know what I think till I see what I say?"

And what happens when we give ourselves the opportunity to do so in the pages of a journal?

There is a great deal of magic involved in this process – the magic of human thought and emotion, of interaction and relationships. Such things are not easily analyzed or calibrated but I have found some interesting information that may help you understand the rich and revelatory benefits of releasing our thoughts and feelings onto the page.

Physiological and Emotional Benefits of Personal Writing

First, let's take a short lesson in physiology. The brain – the seat of our thoughts, memories and emotions – has two parts, two hemispheres. In the vast majority of humans, the left hemisphere is considered the center of logical thought and involved with speech, reading and writing. It tracks time and sequence, and recognizes words, letters and numbers and it sees things by taking them apart, analyzing the pieces. And the right hemisphere, the center of intuitive and creative thought, gathers information from images, and recognizes patterns and spatial forms such as faces, places and objects. It perceives and understands holistically, even metaphorically.

The hemispheres are connected by the corpus callosum, a nerve bundle of 300 million interconnected fibers that passes information back and forth between the two, and then to the rear of the head via the cerebellum, brainstem, which leads to the spinal cord and the rest of the body. In *The Right Mind: Making Sense of the Hemispheres*, Robert Ornstein chronicles the evolutionary history of the human brain and how the hemispheres have come to be responsible for their particular functions. The process is both scientific and mystical, and worthy of deeper study, but for the purpose of this book I can tell you that the essence of his research confirms that when the two centers work together – the left with words (text), the right with images (context), sharing information via the corpus callosum – we are at our best and gratified in an encompassing way. By tracking brain waves, Ornstein discovered that when a person engages in technical writing, only the left hemisphere of the brain is activated, but when writing about thoughts and memories – engaging in the stories of Life with all their images and feelings, both hemispheres are active.

Research also shows that when writing involves the individual's own memories and emotions, the mind/body/spirit is holistically and positively enhanced. James Pennebaker is one of many in the field of psychology who has studied the benefits of writing as a therapeutic tool. He believes that writing about ourselves – particularly the difficulties of our lives – "helps people reorganize their thoughts and feelings [. . .] and create more coherent and meaningful narratives about the events in their lives." (1)

He also postulates that keeping things inside, or secret, is a form of inhibition, and inhibition is known to affect the automatic workings of the body (such as heart beat, breathing, etc.) and the central nervous system as a long term, low level stressor. When we disclose inside information, we reduce inhibition, which reduces this ongoing stress. (2)

Pennebaker conducted extensive studies on groups of people who were asked to write for 15 to 30 minutes each day on assigned topics. Control groups wrote about superficial subjects, such as how they manage their time, while the other groups were given prompts on emotional subjects. Those who worked with personal disclosure showed improved immune function, heightened moods, stress reduction, lowered heart rates, and altered behavior, such as improvement of grades and lower work absenteeism. And, particularly noteworthy is this: the results were non-selective! From senior professionals with advanced degrees to maximum-security prisoners with a 6th grade education, all participants showed comparable emotional and physical benefits.

Everyone benefits from the kind of personal writing a private journal offers – as Theodore Roethke put it, "those who are willing to be vulnerable move among mysteries."

In the late 60's and early 70's diary writing exploded into what we now call "journal writing" and branched out into myriad processes that revealed therapeutic and creative value. During my years of experience with journaling, I have studied many of these methods and techniques, used them, and taught them in journaling and writing workshops.

I often compare these methods and techniques to forms of physical exercise. The more you use them, the stronger your journal writing muscles become. And when used in conjunction with the daily prompts I offer in this book, the easier it will be to allow your thoughts, emotions and ruminations to take shape on the page.

From my personal experience and that of my students, I can assure you that as time goes on the process will become second nature. When you open your journal and put pen to paper, using the techniques that are now hardwired in your brain, the words flow easily in whatever way they choose to come. Like learning to ride a bike, you will look back and wonder how there could have been a time when you didn't know how to do it.

And, just like physical exercise, you will be drawn to a certain process, depending on what you are feeling or challenged by that day. Sometimes a leisurely walk, watching birds and smelling flowers, is preferable to a strenuous hike. Sometimes it's better to weed the garden, rather than dig and plant. Most importantly though: "cross train" your journaling abilities. I encourage you to work over and over again with each of the methods. Become adept in all of them so you can call up what you need to help you find your full expression with ease.

When, Where, How?

When you write in your journal is up to you. Reflect upon your schedule. When do you have 10 to 20 minutes to yourself in a day? Finding the right time can be a circuitous process but absolutely worth the effort.

Here are some creative ways to carve out time, shared by students and workshop participants over the years:

- Get up 15 – 20 minutes earlier than normal to write before the rest of the house wakes.
- On your coffee break at work. Close the door to your office or use ear buds and listen to some ambient music while you write.
- Over lunch
- Traveling on a bus or train
- In the waiting room before an appointment
- Sitting in the car while waiting for someone
- Sitting on the toilet (why not?)
- In the evening, after dinner
- Before going to bed

My best time is first thing in the morning. I write at my desk while I sip my coffee or, if the weather is fine, I write outside. However, mornings were not always good for me, especially when I had two kids to get out the door to school and myself to work. Back then, I took the time when I could get it. The important point is: I took it.

As I did when my children were young, you, too, may need a list of alternatives and take whatever time fits that day's schedule. Or sometimes, a particular writing time works for a while, then life changes so you have to come up with another plan.

The goal is to write every day. But if you can't, don't give up and not write at all. Write when you can, even for 5 minute. And keep at it! Hold your desire to write in your awareness. This is how you will begin to form the habit of writing. And this book's purpose is to give you an easy way into the process every day.

Where you write may very well depend on *when* you write. But if you have the opportunity to choose, I always recommend a place that allows you to commune deeply with your own thoughts. For some that could be anonymously sitting in a coffee shop, for others it must be behind the closed door of a den, office or bathroom. A teenage student once told me that her private place in a house full of people was sitting in the bathtub (not bathing, just sitting), bathroom door locked. It was her favorite place to write. It was her only place to write.

I, also, recommend writing outdoors whenever possible. Energetically speaking, our human vibrational frequency is very close to the Earth's resonance so being in nature can be both soothing and inciting. I find that I am less prone to distraction, more relaxed and often inspired when I write outdoors.

How do you write? I am partial to writing by hand with an instrument I love (mine is a specific, mechanical pencil) in a journal that opens flat, which I have chosen with care, or in one that has been given to me as a gift. The weight of the journal, the smoothness of the pages, lined or un-lined, the cover's décor all play a part in what I choose to use when I start a new journal. The choice is sacred to me and part of the ritual of engaging deeply in the journaling process.

Studies show that the act of writing – thoughts finding their way from the mind, through the heart (speaking metaphorically of our emotions), down the arm and through the hand and fingers to the page – is a powerful and cathartic mind/body process. This is the premise of Julia Cameron's "morning pages" in *The Artist's Way* and G. Lynn Nelson's process in *Writing and Being.* I have studied both thoroughly, used their processes and can attest to the value of their instruction.

However, if you are most comfortable writing at a keyboard, then do it. Just watch for hesitations – meaning that your fingers stop on the keys – as it may indicate that you are editing your thoughts. This can happen with pen/pencil on paper, too. I will address how to work with this issue in my discussion on Free Writing.

Writing Techniques

There are dozens of ways to approach personal, reflective writing. In this book, I am offering the techniques that I have found most beneficial for myself and observed as powerful tools for my clients and journaling students. Each offers a unique way to explore our inner and outer worlds, much like viewing the dimensions of light through various sides of a prism. However, the first technique I share is crucial to all the others. Read on and you will discover why *free writing* is the gateway to our deepest, personal awareness.

Free Writing

Free writing is the heart and soul of journal writing, the unedited, un-judged, openly expressive, unabashed thoughts and feelings you let flow freely from the mind, heart, spirit, subconscious on to the page. The key is to not think about the words that come, but to let them arrive and take you down the river of your mind. By mentally and emotionally creating a degree of separation, you use what is often referred to as the "observer's mind" to be a passenger in the boat of your verbal expressions.

From an early age we are taught to analyze and critique everything – what is safe, what is not; how and when to be polite; when to speak and when to stay silent – the list goes on and on. And we are taught to watch for and correct mistakes immediately, especially when it comes to language and writing. We create boundaries in our mind, which are not bad in and of themselves, as they help protect us, avoid embarrassment, etc., and aid us to function and communicate within the norms of our society.

However, in the privacy of your own thoughts and in the pages of your journal, these do not serve you. Such boundaries do not protect; rather they inhibit and stifle.

The only way to learn to free write is to practice! You must discover how to welcome your words with open arms. To do this, the first task is to get rid of the editor that sits on your shoulder, whispering in your ear such things as ...

You spelled that wrong.
That doesn't make sense.
You have no right to say that.
That's not true.
That sounds stupid.
You don't know what you're talking about.
Your grammar stinks.

These have no place in journal writing. I tell my journaling students, flick that little devil, the Critic, right off your shoulder with, "You're not welcome here. Get lost!"

If need be, create a visualization or a mantra to get rid of the editor/inner critic and use it before you begin to write. Some of my students love the idea of physically flicking their shoulder to remove the Critic. I often do several, deep, cleansing breaths before I write, imaging the Critic being blown farther and farther away from me with each out-breath. You may need to try various approaches to discover what works best for you, then exercise the free will of your mind to Not analyze or critique.

In *The Artist's* Way, Julia Cameron says that her stream-of-consciousness (free) writing exercise, called "morning pages," is "the act of moving the hand across the page and writing down *whatever* comes to mind. Nothing is too petty, to silly, too stupid, or too weird to be included … (this) gets us to the other side: the other side of our fear, our negativity, of our moods. Above all, they get us beyond our Censor. Beyond the reach of the Censor's babble, we find our own quiet center, the place where we hear the still, small voice that is at once our creator's and our own." (3)

Because you are working to change a negative thought pattern with this technique, your writing may feel labored at first but it will get easier and easier. As you master silencing the critic and using your observer's mind, you will begin to feel the exhilaration that comes from freedom of expression. Great understanding and deep insights can arise from this freedom.

To begin your free writing practice, start with a 5-minute write. Set a timer and persist with the following instructions:

With the editor off your shoulder, begin writing by copying the prompt into your journal and then without lifting your pen from the page, start writing the first thing that comes to your mind in response to the prompt – No Matter What It Is! – and keep your pen moving with words and thoughts – No Matter What They Are! – remember, NO EDITOR. If your mind goes blank, still keep your pen to the page and scribble, make circles, or doodle until another word or thought (any word or thought) comes and continue to write from there until the timer goes off.

Practice writing for 5 minutes for 2 or 3 days and then increase incrementally to 10, 15 or 20 minutes. Don't wait too long to increase your writing time. I promise, you won't hurt yourself. You will be expanding yourself.

In lieu of doing timed writing, you can do "page writing." Using the same free writing instructions, write non-stop until you come to the end of the page. Write only one page for several days and then increase to 1 ½ or 2 pages, 3 pages or more!

Soon you will forget about the timer or the number of pages and just write what you are meant to write. Your Higher Self's need for expression will be your gauge. Free writing can be used – and should be practiced – with every other technique I share in this book, as it is the purest path to the richness of your inner thoughts and feelings.

My mentor and friend, G. Lynn Nelson, shares in his book, *Writing and Being*, "So our words must be born in our hearts and find their way to our heads. We must begin with our feelings. Feelings are where our words become flesh […] That is where you enter the river […] say your anger – swear and scream in your journal. Say your hurt, your sorrow, your grief – cry in your journal. Say your fears – let your journal have them. When I use my journal in these ways […] I have a little more room inside to breathe, a little more room for feelings of love for myself and others." (4)

Word Mining

Word mining is an effective companion technique to free writing. Here's how it works.

Upon completing a page or two of writing in response to the day's prompt, close your journal, close your eyes and breathe deeply, clearing your mind of thoughts, letting them go with the out-breath and letting your physical body relax. Take about 10 breaths in this way.

Now, open your journal. Read what you just wrote and, as you do so, circle the words that jump off the page and draw your attention. You may circle only a couple or you may circle a dozen – just stay true to circling what attracts you.

On a new page of your journal, write the circled words in a single column down the page.

Once again, close your eyes and take several, deep, cleansing breaths. When you open your eyes, scan the column. What *single word* jumps off the page and draws your attention?

Write that word on a new page and immediately begin to free write for 5 minutes. Many journalers find it helpful to start this write with word associations. For example, if the word you choose is "blue" begin quickly and freely writing what you associate with blue – sky, water, sadness, black and blue, bubble gum ... until an imagine or phrase finds its way to the page, then continue allowing your thoughts and feelings to expand from there.

When you finish writing, check in with yourself. Do you feel clear? Do you feel disturbed? Do you feel unfinished? If you feel unfinished, apply the word mining technique to the second writing.

Word mining is like working up the garden of our thoughts and offers a subtle yet powerful way to open the subconscious. Those words that attract you hold greater meaning than their dictionary definitions. They have unconscious feelings and memories attached to them. When you write *into* these words and release their greater meaning into conscious thought, your personal awareness can increase greatly. You will begin to see yourself through a different side of the prism *and* gain understanding of why you think, feel, act and react as you do.

This can be a painful or joyful process. But, think of it this way – when we recall and release our painful experiences we offer healing to our mind/body/spirit, and when we remember and reflect upon our joys, we nurture ourselves with love.

Use word mining with any technique when you have an "unfinished" feeling about your journal entry. And it works just as well – sometimes even more dramatically – if you leave the journal entry unread for a couple of hours or even days. Go back to it when you can or feel ready and "word mine" it. Sometimes the subconscious needs extra time to open and be willing to let go of its secrets.

Powerful Questions

In the late 1970s, two English professors, Linda Trichter Metcalf and Tobin Simon, developed a writing technique called "Proprioceptive Writing" in which one writes freely by candlelight for 25 minutes, listening to slow tempo Baroque music, the beat resonant to the human pulse. Like the free writing technique I discussed previously, the writer keeps pen to page letting thoughts come as they choose. But in this method, if one gets stuck or curious, he/she writes the proprioceptive question, "What do I mean by …?" and then continues to write a response. This question and response technique helps to keep the writing process going and deepen one's engagement.

Metcalf and Tobin say of this process, "Writing is not the end of the practice but rather the means to gain insight into and power over how we live and think […] Over time it strengthens our sense of self and connects us to the world." (5)

If you want to learn more about Metcalf and Tobin's work, please refer to *Writing the Mind Alive*, which is in my bibliography. For the purposes of this book, I want to introduce you to the practice of using powerful questions like theirs. "What do I mean by …?" or "Why did I say …?" offer ways of dissecting abstract words to get to their true meaning for you.

Consider words like love, fear, hate, confused, important or difficult. These are intangible words. We all can relate to their universal or theoretical meaning, but such words actually manifest experientially in very different ways for each individual and, thus, *meaning* becomes completely subjective.

So, for example, by asking questions like "What do I mean by confused?" or "Why do I think I'm confused?" I can begin to deconstruct that word into experiences and feelings that are specific to *me*. I am not allowing myself to hide behind these abstract words, but rather examining them deeply to transform them into concrete information born out of my own life. And when

I uncover this information, I am bringing insight to my Self and greater awareness of how I interact with the world.

Once again, powerful questioning is an enlightening, companion technique to the others I share in this book.

Letter Writing

In an age where texting and email reign as two of our main forms of interpersonal communication, letter writing is a novel experience for many people. However, for hundreds of years, the letter has been the most personal, private and attentive way people shared the experiences of their lives and expressed their deepest feelings to another.

Without knowing the psychological and physical benefits of writing about meaningful experiences and sharing thoughts and feelings, people were engaging in a powerful, cathartic process.

Letter writing in your journal offers you the opportunity to speak your mind and heart to someone without reserve, knowing that at the end of it you can sign off and close your journal. The information has been relayed, the experiences shared, the feelings expressed without having to fold the pages, put them in an envelope, stamp and send.

Several prompts in this book ask you specifically to engage in letter writing. However, you can use letter writing with any prompt response if you come up against a potent feeling or unresolved issue. Examples might be: a lost love, someone who has passed on, a broken relationship, a long, lost friend, a grumpy boss or a checked-out co-worker. Or, you may choose to write a letter to an aspect of your Self: the child you once were, the inner child you carry with you now, your sadness, you unhappiness or your powerful Self.

The key is to express to "whomever" exactly what you need to say, without reservation.

Energetically speaking, when we hold within us unexpressed thoughts and feelings about another – good or bad – they can keep us unduly attached to that person or affect our energy exchange with others.

Here are two examples: If I have not released old feelings for a past love, this can affect my ability to offer love fully to someone new. Or, if I am holding on to unexpressed anger towards someone, that anger can leak out into other important relationships in my life.

I am not purporting that if you write a letter to someone, you will be completely clear and released of thoughts and emotions concerning them, and that will be the end of it. I am saying that by giving voice on the page to what is unexpressed in you – good or bad – you will expand your awareness of what holds you back *and* what can move you forward to living a healthier, more balanced life. Letter writing is a tool to help you discover that awareness.

Writing in the Third Person (he/she)

When we shift out of First Person "I" writing into Third Person "he or she" writing, we offer ourselves a degree of separation from the deeply personal "I" experience and write our thoughts from what is considered the omniscient (God) point of view, or we can think of it as using the "observer's mind."

This is a highly effective point of view because we are looking at the issues of our life from a completely different angle of the prism. In my experience, third person writing offers a couple of interesting insights.

First, imagine what it would be like to watch a situation that has challenged you play out as if it were a movie reel: you observing your own behavior. Certainly it would be a very different occurrence than walking in your shoes, being in your skin. And that different point of view can shed some light on aspects that you could not see from your "I" perspective.

Secondly, that omniscient viewpoint often has enlightening things to contribute about your feelings, actions or words concerning that situation. This can segue into the insights of your Higher Self, Spirit or God Knowledge.

The third person viewpoint is one you don't normally take because, let's face it, for the most part, life is a very subjective affair! So, it can be quite liberating for you, as the "omniscient" writer, to speak freely about what you observe. What finds its way to the page may be critical, comforting, provocative, directive or any number of things, especially if you allow yourself to engage in the all important, free writing process.

Dialogue

A dialogue can be between you and a person (or issue) you love, hate, miss, or for which you have unresolved feelings. It can be between you and an aspect of yourself, your body, an emotion, an object – whatever or whomever you choose. Writing a conversation between any two things can be a deeply informative way of helping you discover another perspective or uncover your own thoughts and feelings about someone or a particular experience.

Throughout the book, you will find several prompts that ask you to engage in a particular dialogue. However, this can be a helpful technique to inject into a free writing response to any prompt in order to expand awareness of your Self and your world.

You can initiate the conversation with a question or give voice to the other with a statement or question, to which you then respond. Refrain from writing out, "I said" or "he said" as this will slow down the dialogue. Instead, whenever you change voices, start a new line. Write quickly and let the words flow without editing, just as you do in free writing, and continue until you feel the conversation is done. This may mean that you feel some sense of resolution or it may simply feel finished.

Resolved or not, I guarantee you will be well informed by the exchange, as the process opens the door to the subconscious and, some say, even to other worlds. Remember that what comes to the page is a gift from your Higher Self. Don't edit or over-analyze, rather use what you have written to expand your understanding of You.

Writing With Your Non-Dominant Hand

To further deepen the dialogue process, use your non-dominant hand in the exchange. In my experience, this is most effective when you are struggling with an aspect of yourself. With your dominant hand, write in your normal way, using your normal writing "voice" on the page. Then, switch and use your non-dominant hand to respond.

This is very challenging for many of us because we are not adept at much of anything with the "other" hand, let alone using it to write! But the non-dominate hand can be amazingly honest and forthright, when given the opportunity to have its say, as it is believed to stimulate parts of the brain not normally used for writing. Journalers who are willing to give space on the page to this kind of dialogue most often find the conversations to be short, but very powerful and revealing.

Once again, this technique can be used during any prompt response and can elicit a particularly potent and interesting exchange when used with powerful questioning.

Lists

I use list making a lot in my own journaling process and ask many of my coaching clients to use it, as well. Several prompts in this book ask you to list things, which is a wonderful way to heighten awareness or get to the heart of a matter.

For example, if my client is centered on what is not going right in her life, I will ask her to make a list of what *is* going right. This helps shift negative thinking to positive thinking. Thus, a list of accomplishments, of things you are grateful for, of good qualities you have, of supportive people in your life, of blessings you feel, all serve to bring attention to the goodness in and around you.

Once the burden of negative thinking is lifted, even a little, often times what you thought was bad isn't quite so, and you have created more positive mental space to find solutions to the aspects of life that aren't working as you'd like.

You can use a list to brainstorm solutions or discover pros and cons. From a list, you might want to choose one item and explore it deeply. Or, consider interjecting a list in your writing response as a way of answering a powerful, proprioceptive kind of question. Even try using a list within a list!

Recently I made a list of several concerns I had. After writing one down, I made a sub-list of possible remedies, then went on to the next concern and again sub-listed several solutions. When I was done, I felt relieved to know that I had options – several of them, in fact – and that I could go back to my journal later to review and choose which would be viable to implement.

Lists can be written in bullet points, using phrases, or elaborated in sentences or paragraphs. Write the way you want to write to get what you need out of your head and heart onto the page.

Remember, how can you know what you think till you see what you say?

How to Refer to Your Journal Writing

When you write, you may have instant insights or glean important information about your world and you Self. But there will be times when it will take your subconscious a while to process what you have revealed or mulled over on the page. So be prepared to let your words just be there and trust that your intuition will take you back to what you need to revisit.

Sometimes I don't read what I've written until the last page of the journal has been filled. Only then will I set aside some quiet time to read and reflect on its contents. Often I find myself amazed at the wisdom and insight of my own words or I can see the evolution of my thoughts, which helped me solve a problem or reach a goal. I come to recognize what kinds of situations have provoked anxiety or fear for me. And, many times I discover what Virginia Wolff calls "shivering fragments" – the seeds of creative work hoping to come into fullness.

Certainly, I also refer to my journal at any time I've made a list of "to-do's" or if I want to transcribe something to use in a piece of creative or inspirational writing. Sometimes I don't feel that I've fully worked out a problem I'm facing, so I'll go back and read what I've written previously on the issue to provoke more conversation with myself.

Note that some of the prompts in this book specifically ask you to go back and read what you wrote. This is part of the self-reflection process and is meant to help you discover how what you've written previously can increase your awareness and move you forward.

Some of my students like to read what they wrote from the previous day before they begin a new write. Others re-read weekly or monthly. Whatever you choose, I encourage you to do so at some point. As I mentioned above from my own experience you, too, will be amazed at the wisdom and insights of your own words. And often, when you choose to review your journal it is timely, with an epiphany there on the page before you.

All the answers are within us, my friends. We just have to be willing to search the archives of our Higher Self to find them.

It's Time to Begin!

Now you have the tools to begin your journaling journey. There are several ways to use these prompts:

- Start at the beginning and work your way through, from 1 to 365.
- Open to any page and use whichever prompt catches your eye first.
- Don't use the prompt, per se ~ merely reading it may compel you to write about something else that is more pressing or important. Go for it!
- Download the *Your Journal Companion* app for iOS and Android devices from the App Store or Google Play Store – it will alert you with the day's prompt at a time you choose, or use the shuffle feature for a surprise prompt.

Whatever way you choose, you may find that on some occasions the prompt before you doesn't feel right, annoys you or deeply challenges you.

If it doesn't feel right, trust your instinct and move on to the next or another prompt. Your Higher Self may have something else it wants to talk about that day.

However, if the prompt annoys or challenges you, I encourage you to stick with it. Give me a talking to about the stupidity of the prompt, if you must, but write into it anyway. It may be that you are hitting what I call "pay dirt" which idiomatically means you are about to discover something important and of value to you.

I'll give you an example from my own life of how the journaling process can help you solve the challenges you face. (Interestingly, this example occurred during the writing of this book.) Notice how many of the processes discussed in these pages I used to discover my issue and its solution. My writing "muscles" are well developed, so these came to me naturally, in the order that supported the best exploration of my problem. As you strengthen your writing muscles through focused practice of the techniques, this will be so for you, also.

I set aside some time from my normal schedule to concentrate on the book while spending the summer months in California. My husband and I rented a lovely, little cottage near the ocean. Our plan: I would settle in with our two kitties, and my husband would commute from work in Arizona for long weekends. Our two sons live in California and each is about an hour's drive from the cottage, so I expected plenty of comings and goings for dinner, overnights and extended weekend stays, and in between I would work on the book. A perfect scenario! And for two weeks that is exactly how it went.

And then, Life happened. My husband had to cancel two weekend stays due to a critical business project, and both of my sons got bombarded with work and personal commitments. Though my days were busy and productive, I found myself feeling quite conflicted and empty in the evenings. A few nights of that began to disturb the flow of my days and affect my work on the writing project. So, as I do every morning, I went to my journal with the intention of exploring the nature of this empty feeling and how I could change it.

I started out with this: "I am not sure what I need to write this morning – I am feeling a bit of conflict … not conflict, I think I am feeling a bit lonely.

And there it was, in the first line of my writing. Loneliness.

The next four pages of my journal included several proprioceptive questions like, "What do you mean by lonely?" to discover what practically encompassed that abstract word for me. This led into a dialogue with my Self about those practical aspects. Once I began to have clarity about the feeling, I could release it. I sensed the denseness of the "aloneness" literally leaving my body, which freed my mental and emotional energy to brainstorm solutions to this challenge.

I came up with a list of fun, creative things I could do on my own in the evenings – some at the cottage, others required me to go out into the world. The list was great. I felt liberated by it, but also knew that I needed motivation to implement the "doing" part of it.

So, I made activity cards, writing each item from the list on a separate index card. I decided that everyday, in the late afternoon, I would shuffle the cards, pick one and do it that evening! I committed myself to the project.

Two important things happened from my journal exploration:

1. I learned more about myself, about the nature of aloneness and how it affects me.
2. I affirmed to myself that I have the answers to my challenges within me. I found ways to enjoy my evenings on my own, and more importantly, the activities on my list proved to bring great richness and a lot of fun into my life.

Journaling for self-awareness and personal discovery is a layered process. When we first begin, we scratch the surface of our inner understanding. As we build our writing muscles, using the techniques offered in this book, we learn to dig deeper, turn the soil, pull the weeds and find the roots of our thoughts and feelings.

Be courageous and bold in your writing, because the more you learn about yourself, the more power and choices you have to issue positive change in your life.

365 Prompts

(For convenience consider using the Your Journal Companion app)

~ 1 ~

What's missing in my life is …

~ 2 ~

I am courageous when …

~ 3 ~

I listen most closely to my heart when …

~ 4 ~

I feel vulnerable …

~ 5 ~

I wish that … but I accept that …

~ 6 ~

The greatest accomplishment in my life so far …

~ 7 ~

I can love myself more …

~ 8 ~

When I was a child I loved …
Explore why. Do you still love this? Why?

~ 9 ~

I thought I failed when … but now I realize …

~ 10 ~

When I need support and encouragement I can turn to …
explore who, what and why.

~ 11 ~

I feel wise when …

~ 12 ~

Life feels hard when …

~ 13 ~

I never told anyone …

~ 14 ~

Write a love letter to your Self.
(Don't be embarrassed, write from the heart
and in a the way that you would write to someone else.)

~ 15 ~

I am grateful for …
(list 10 things)

~ 16 ~

Today, my time is best invested in ...

~ 17 ~

What treasure (skill, ability, knowledge, etc.)
do you have within you that you have not yet shared
with the world? Why is it a treasure?
How can you begin to share it?

~ 18 ~

The best way for me to lift the sadness I feel in my life is ...

~ 19 ~

Who and what nurture you? Explore why and how.

~ 20 ~

I can bring better health into my life by …

~ 21 ~

Write a letter to your pain (physical or emotional).

~ 22 ~

Write for 5 minutes, starting with "I believe ..."
Then switch to your non-dominant hand and continue
writing from where you left off for 5 minutes.
Now, write about the experience of this exercise.

~ 23 ~

To be fully alive right now, I ...

~ 24 ~

I trust my intuition to tell me ...

~ 25 ~

I can live my own life by …

~ 26 ~

I am a perfectionist when it comes to …
Why? How does this serve, or hinder, me?

~ 27 ~

If I could change one thing about my past …

~ 28 ~

Write a letter to a grandparent or elder person from whom
you have learned an important life lesson or value,
recounting when and how he/she impacted you.

~ 29 ~

I am avoiding ...

~ 30 ~

Do I embrace change, or do I fear it? Explore why.

~ 31 ~

I can make more time for myself by ... (list 5 things).
Which one can you implement immediately?
Write a contract with yourself about when and how often.

~ 32 ~

I limit myself when ...

~ 33 ~

I am sick and tired of always being the one ...
After free writing about this, brainstorm solutions with,
"I can change this by ..."

~ 34 ~

I feel at home when …

~ 35 ~

A week from now I want …

~ 36 ~

Write about the last time you had an "ah-ha" moment.
How has it changed you?

~ 37 ~

Step outdoors or go to an open window.
Set a timer for 2 minutes, then close your eyes,
breathe deeply and listen for the sounds of Nature.
Free write in response to this experience.

~ 38 ~

I feel safe when ...

~ 39 ~

The most meaningful gift I ever received ...

~ 40 ~

Today my heart feels ... Why?

~ 41 ~

With whom do you need to reconcile?
Free write about the issue that divided you and then
make a list of possible ways you can remedy the situation.

~ 42 ~

I can make peace with my body ...

~ 43 ~

I remember a time when I felt really lost …

~ 44 ~

To have a spiritual practice means …

~ 45 ~

I yearn for …

~ 46 ~

My favorite scent is … Why?

~ 47 ~

Am I going in the right direction? Explore why or why not.

~ 48 ~

I want to forget …

~ 49 ~

One day I want to be able to tell my grandchildren that …

~ 50 ~

List your accomplishments from yesterday.
What are you most satisfied by? Why?

~ 51 ~

Recall a magical experience in your life.
Describe it and explore why it was magical for you.

~ 52 ~

What do I really want to do that I won't let myself enjoy?
Why?

~ 53 ~

I am most proud of ... Why?

~ 54 ~

I feel empty when ...

~ 55 ~

Use all of your senses (sight, hearing, taste, touch, smell)
to describe what love means to you.

~ 56 ~

My Authentic Self wants to tell me ...

~ 57 ~

In order to grow as a person, I must let go of ...

~ 58 ~

I simply cannot …

~ 59 ~

I can get on with my life …

~ 60 ~

With whom do you have the most difficult relationship?
What makes it so? How can you begin to change this?

~ 61 ~

I am most relaxed when …

~ 62 ~

Write a letter to the child you once were and tell him/her
the important things you've learned since then.

~ 63 ~

I am happy to be …

~ 64 ~

In your mind, review the last few days.
Who showed you kindness, what did he/she do,
and how did it make you feel? Reflect on the
importance of this experience.

~ 65 ~

If I could change only one thing in my life, I would ...

~ 66 ~

Sometimes I am afraid to ask for help because ...

~ 67 ~

I can listen to and honor my own inner wisdom by …

~ 68 ~

Make a list of your positive qualities. Make a second list
of the positive qualities you want to possess.
How can you begin to bring those qualities into your life?

~ 69 ~

What challenges me about my life right now is …

~ 70 ~

I wallowed in self-pity when … How did you get out of it?

~ 71 ~

When I look out the window…

~ 72 ~

I am having a problem with …
Why? What can you do to remedy this?

~ 73 ~

I can simplify my life by …

~ 74 ~

Write a letter of gratefulness to your best teacher.

~ 75 ~

What put-downs do you say to yourself? Make a list of them.
Now, challenge each of them with a positive affirmation
about yourself.

~ 76 ~

When I close my eyes, I feel …

~ 77 ~

I can recover from exhaustion by …

~ 78 ~

I miss …

~ 79 ~

What habit have you changed? Why?
How did you change it?

~ 80 ~

Use all of your senses (sight, hearing, taste, touch, smell)
to describe what hate means to you.

~ 81 ~

This week I am most proud …

~ 82 ~

What does home mean to you?

~ 83 ~

Imagine that you have a guardian angel. Name and describe
your angel. Let yourself free write about what your
angel might like to tell you.

~ 84 ~

My passion in life is ... and I can support my passion by ...

~ 85 ~

I am feeling …

~ 86 ~

I am a loner when …

~ 87 ~

A month from now I want …

~ 88 ~

What makes you feel anxious? Where do you feel it
in your body? If that part of your body could talk,
what would it tell you?

~ 89 ~

I can feed my soul/spirit/center by ...

~ 90 ~

Free write, starting with, "I am ..." (make a list of 12 things).
Upon finishing, reflect on each "I am ..." Which of the 12
most clearly represents your Authentic Self? Explore why.

~ 91 ~

What habit do you carry from your mother?
How has it helped or hindered you?

~ 92 ~

With whom do you have the most loving relationship?
What makes it so?

~ 93 ~

I am most true to myself when …

~ 94 ~

What challenges your courage? How? Why?
What can you do to change this?

~ 95 ~

I am out of my comfort zone when …
Why? I can change this by …

~ 96 ~

It is hard for me to be alone …

~ 97 ~

Three things I hold dear to me are ... Why?

~ 98 ~

Reflect on the last few days. With whom did you have a conflict? Write about what happened. Now, write about how you solved the conflict or could solve it.

~ 99 ~

When I smell ... it reminds me ...

~ 100 ~

What has been your greatest mistake? Your greatest success?
How do they differ? What makes them similar?

~ 101 ~

I can be content with what I have by …

~ 102 ~

I feel most at home, spiritually, when I …

~ 103 ~

I have always wanted to …

~ 104 ~

I believe …

~ 105 ~

The aspect of Nature that nurtures me most is … Why?

~ 106 ~

What habit do you want to change?
Explore why, and how you can do so.

~ 107 ~

Write a letter of comfort and love to the child you once were,
who endured hardship or suffering.

~ 108 ~

Today I am grateful for ... Make a list and explore
why you are grateful.

~ 109 ~

I feel powerful when …

~ 110 ~

I unconditionally love _____ (a person, place or thing). Why? How do you show this love?

~ 111 ~

I really want to fix …

~ 112 ~

I feel open and truly alive when …

~ 113 ~

I want to reconcile within myself …

~ 114 ~

I remember when …

~ 115 ~

What do I still trust as I did when I was a child? Why?

~ 116 ~

Have a dialogue with your internal critic.
What is it saying to you? What do you want to tell it?

~ 117 ~

I can "live" gratitude by …

~ 118 ~

Recall a dream you had recently. What image or emotion
stands out from the dream? Write it down and allow
yourself to free write from that point.

~ 119 ~

Today I am challenged …
Why? List 3 possible solutions to this challenge.

~ 120 ~

I imagine …

~ 121 ~

If I got really quiet, I could figure out ...

~ 122 ~

I accept ... because ...

~ 123 ~

I want to help ... Why?

~ 124 ~

Three things I want to let go of are … Why?

~ 125 ~

How do you feed your soul?

~ 126 ~

Who has loved you unconditionally? How? Why?

~ 127 ~

Do I associate "home" with a person, a place, a way of being? What does home mean to me? Explore Home.

~ 128 ~

I am a team player when …

~ 129 ~

I have the most fun when …

~ 130 ~

I like to be alone …

~ 131 ~

I am in the dark about …
How can you bring light to this darkness?

~ 132 ~

Make a list of your talents and skills.
Which are you not using? Why? How can you make
them active in your life? (Be creative!)

~ 133 ~

Being the oldest/middle/youngest child in my family
has helped and hindered me in the following ways ...
(List and explore why.)

~ 134 ~

Five years from now I want ...

~ 135 ~

What and who do I hate? Why?

~ 136 ~

What part of yourself are you neglecting right now? Why?
What can you do to remedy this?

~ 137 ~

To expand my spiritual growth, I can ...

~ 138 ~

_____ brings me so much joy. Explore how and why.

~ 139 ~

It's time that I …

~ 140 ~

I lost my innocence when …

~ 141 ~

Today my intention is …

~ 142 ~

What do you seek?

~ 143 ~

How can I be content with who I am?

~ 144 ~

What or whom do you call your beloved? Why?

~ 145 ~

I confess …

~ 146 ~

I can bring balance to my life …

~ 147 ~

I can be a better friend …

~ 148 ~

I want to believe …

~ 149 ~

Have a dialogue with your Inner Child.

~ 150 ~

If I had only one story to tell about my life …

~ 151 ~

Who has been a hero in your life?
Write a letter of gratefulness to that person.

~ 152 ~

My inner guidance is telling me …

~ 153 ~

I would die for … Why?

~ 154 ~

When I close my eyes, I hear …

~ 155 ~

I believe in …

~ 156 ~

This week I applaud myself for …

~ 157 ~

The hardest thing for me to listen to …

~ 158 ~
Write a letter to someone who has always been there for you,
recounting when and how he/she made a difference in your life.
If you can't think of anyone who has done this, write a letter
to the person you wished had been there for you.

~ 159 ~

The things that are essential to my well-being are …
(make a list). Are these things active in your life now?
If not, how can you make them so?

~ 160 ~

When I was a child, I was afraid of …
Explore why. Are you still afraid of this? Why?

~ 161 ~

Where do I feel most at home?

~ 162 ~

I feel ashamed …

~ 163 ~

I want to accept …

~ 164 ~

Where do you feel pain or tension in your body right now?
Have a dialogue with your body to find out why.
Ask it for a solution?

~ 165 ~

Dear _____, It may comfort you to know …

~ 166 ~

Read your journal entry from 7 days ago.
Explore what has changed for you since then.

~ 167 ~

The most intense relationship in my life is/was …
Why? How does/did the relationship help, or hinder, me?

~ 168 ~

Consider a problem you can't seem to solve.
What would your best friend advise you to do? Write a
dialogue between you and this friend, and discuss options.

~ 169 ~

I am disappointed in …

~ 170 ~

The best memory of my life …

~ 171 ~

How can I live my true calling in life?

~ 172 ~

As long as I am on this earth …

~ 173 ~

I am grateful for … (list at least 10 things)

~ 174 ~

What has been the best experience of your life so far?
First, recall it on the page; then explore the
feelings this brings up for you.

~ 175 ~

Who has been a good teacher in your life?
What did he/she/it teach you? How did he/she/it teach you?

~ 176 ~

I can relieve the stress in my life by ... (list 6 ways)
Explore how you can incorporate them into your daily life.

~ 177 ~

I have great faith in ... Why?

~ 178 ~

My favorite time of year is ... Explore why?

~ 179 ~

I thought my life had ended when ... but now I know ...

~ 180 ~

I appreciate myself today ...

~ 181 ~

I want to learn how to … and I can start by …

~ 182 ~

I am happy when …

~ 183 ~

To my relationships I bring …

~ 184 ~

Write a letter to your body.

~ 185 ~

I feel empowered …

~ 186 ~

Have a dialogue with your Creator.

~ 187 ~

I may not be … but I am …

~ 188 ~

All I want to do right now is …

~ 189 ~

_____ doesn't bother me because …

~ 190 ~

The first time I …

~ 191 ~

I feel inspired and creative when …

~ 192 ~

Regarding my cultural heritage, I feel …

~ 193 ~

Who in your life do you respect? What have they done to
earn your respect? What key quality do they have?
Do you have or want this quality?

~ 194 ~

Write a letter to someone you no longer have a relationship
with and share everything that went unsaid before
you parted ways.

~ 195 ~

Open your journal to any previous page and read the entry.
Free write about what you wrote then.

~ 196 ~

I am obedient to … Does this benefit or stifle you?

~ 197 ~

My greatest gift to the world …

~ 198 ~

I can create more health in my life …

~ 199 ~

I am a good friend because …

~ 200 ~

Write a letter to your heart.

~ 201 ~

I want to put more energy towards …

~ 202 ~

Of all the roles you play in life – partner, sibling, artist, athlete, etc. – which role are you neglecting but would like to cultivate? Why are you neglecting it? How can you change this?

~ 203 ~

I am ashamed …

~ 204 ~

Right now my spiritual condition is … Why?

~ 205 ~

Read your journal entry from 30 days ago.
How have you or your circumstances changed since then?

~ 206 ~

I forgive ...

~ 207 ~

I can accept the imperfections in myself by ...

~ 208 ~

I forgot that I love … (make a list).
Explore why you forgot these things.

~ 209 ~

Close your eyes and think about your family.
What comes to your mind ~ a particular memory, a feeling …?
Start writing with, "When I think of my family …"

~ 210 ~

I accept …

~ 211 ~

I am confident in …

~ 212 ~

When you have a disagreement with someone, how do you handle it? Does this serve you? If it does, why? If not, brainstorm ways you can change your approach.

~ 213 ~

Write a dialogue between you and your greatest fear.

~ 214 ~

I am comfortable/uncomfortable in my body because …

~ 215 ~

Now I … back then, I …

~ 216 ~

I am not a good friend when …

~ 217 ~

I hope …

~ 218 ~

Free write about a challenge you are facing right now; then make a list of resources (people, education, etc.) that can help you remedy the situation.

~ 219 ~

Consider all the roles you play in life ~ daughter/son, co-worker, boss, parent, etc. In which role are you the least comfortable? Explore why?

~ 220 ~

Who have I forsaken? Explore how and why?

~ 221 ~

Find a quiet place, sit comfortably or lie down, close your eyes
and listen to the silence for 5 or 10 minutes. (use a timer)
If an obtrusive noise comes, accept it and let it pass.
Engage with the silence. When the time is up, free write
from the stillness that you felt inside you.

~ 222 ~

Go back to your journal entry from 30 days ago.
Read what you wrote. What has changed (or not changed)
for you since then? Explore why.

~ 223 ~

I help myself to be more balanced and calm by ...
(list 10 things). Which one works best? Why?
Which one do you want to do more often? Why?

~ 224 ~

What object have you kept for a long time? Describe it,
where it came from and explore why it is important to you.

~ 225 ~

Yesterday I wanted ... but today ... Explore why?

~ 226 ~

I feel … I need … I want …
Reflect on what you have written.

~ 227 ~

I love and appreciate …

~ 228 ~

Who have you had a disagreement with recently?
Close your eyes and imagine being in their skin, walking
in their shoes. Write a letter to you from their point of view.

~ 229 ~

The traits I dislike in myself are ... (make a list).
I dislike them because ... I can begin to change them by ...

~ 230 ~

What I love about my life right now ...

~ 231 ~

Write a dialogue between you and your pain
(physical or emotional).

~ 232 ~

My best physical attribute is ...
How does this attribute serve you?

~ 233 ~

When I grow older, I want to look back and say ...

~ 234 ~

If I could be an aspect of Nature (a mountain, the ocean,
a tree, the wind, etc.), I would be ... Why?

~ 235 ~

I have always wanted to … Why?

~ 236 ~

I am grateful for … Why?

~ 237 ~

Why didn't I …?

~ 238 ~

I have compassion for ...

~ 239 ~

I hate the smell of ... Explore why.

~ 240 ~

What basic truths do you live by?
Make a list and explore why each truth is a truth for you.

~ 241 ~

Write a dialogue between you and someone,
whom you loved, who has died.

~ 242 ~

The biggest challenge I am facing right now is _____.
Explore why this is challenging and brainstorm a list
of possible solutions.

~ 243 ~

Right now I feel …

~ 244 ~

If I could transform into an animal, I would become ...
Why? What does this tell you about yourself?

~ 245 ~

I acknowledge myself for ...

~ 246 ~

Unconditional love means ...

~ 247 ~

For me to change the way I think about _____ I can …

~ 248 ~

What am I when I am empty?

~ 249 ~

Why did I …?

~ 250 ~

The same old tape keeps playing in my head. It says …
but the truth is …

~ 251 ~

This week I accomplished … (list at least 10 things)

~ 252 ~

What or where is your most tranquil place? Why?
Explore how you can take that tranquility into your daily life.

~ 253 ~

Have you dealt with or are you currently dealing with a
physical issue? Explore how this issue made/makes you feel.
What have you learned from it?

~ 254 ~

_____ (person or event) taught me an important
life lesson. Explore what you learned and how.
Why is it important to you?

~ 255 ~

What habit do you carry from your father?
How has it helped or hindered you?

~ 256 ~

If I believe I am enough, then how must I live my life?

~ 257 ~

Go outside and truly look at your surroundings.
What object attracts your eye? If the object is portable,
hold it in your hands; if not, place your hands on it.
Close your eyes and listen to what the object is saying.
Go back to your journal and write what it is telling you.

~ 258 ~

I feel powerless when ...

~ 259 ~

Write a letter to your Authentic Self.

~ 260 ~

If I could, I would bring _____ back to life.
Why? How would this serve you?

~ 261 ~

Today I am grateful for ...

~ 262 ~

Make a list of assumptions you have about yourself.
Affirm or refute each of them. Or if one stands out,
free write about that assumption.

~ 263 ~

I experience the Divine/God/Spirit moving in me when ...

~ 264 ~

What I value most in this life is ... and I reflect these
values back into the world ...

~ 265 ~

I want to change …

~ 266 ~

The most important thing in my life …

~ 267 ~

Compassion means …

~ 268 ~

I am afraid …

~ 269 ~

Use all of your senses (sight, hearing, taste, touch, smell)
to describe your greatest joy.

~ 270 ~

I can bring peace into my life …

~ 271 ~

If _____ (a person) were with me right now,
he/she would tell me ...

~ 272 ~

I remember when I thought I wanted ... but now I realize ...

~ 273 ~

Ten things I value in myself are ... Explore each one.

~ 274 ~

In your mind, review the last few days. To whom
did you show kindness, what did you do, and how did it
make you feel? Reflect on the importance of this experience.

~ 275 ~

Today my heart wants to say ...

~ 276 ~

What recent event deeply impacted you? How? Why?
Does it need action or resolution? How? Why?

~ 277 ~

What part of you has been silenced? How? Why? Can you let that part begin to speak again? How will you do this?

~ 278 ~

The most important person in my life ...

~ 279 ~

How can I be content with where I am?

~ 280 ~

I wish …

~ 281 ~

Who annoyed you or made you mad recently?
Free write from that person's perspective.

~ 282 ~

What lie do you tell yourself? Explore how, when and why.

~ 283 ~

What have I forsaken? Explore why.

~ 284 ~

I can accept the imperfections in others by …

~ 285 ~

I can be a better daughter/son/sibling by …

~ 286 ~

How can I practice compassion at home?

~ 287 ~

I miss _____ (person, place or thing).
Write him/her/it a letter.

~ 288 ~

Count 14 journal entries back from today.
Read what you wrote. What single word stands out? Begin
free writing from that word for 10 minutes without stopping.

~ 289 ~

I remember …

~ 290 ~

If I got really quiet, I would see …

~ 291 ~

I am comfortable/uncomfortable about my sexuality
because/when …

~ 292 ~

I can bring happiness into my life ...

~ 293 ~

Close your eyes. Take 3 easy, deep breaths and be still.
Listen to your heart. Free write what it tells you.

~ 294 ~

I have never revealed ...

~ 295 ~

What part of you feels powerful? Why? How?

~ 296 ~

Something that has always haunted me ... Explore why.

~ 297 ~

Yesterday, I wish ...

~ 298 ~

What parts of my Self are literally and/or metaphorically
killing me? How can I remedy this?

~ 299 ~

My power comes from … How and when do I use my power?

~ 300 ~

My true calling in life is … Explore why.

~ 301 ~

What do I hold closest to my heart? Why?

~ 302 ~

Where do you feel pain or tension in your body right now?
Have a dialogue with your body to find out why.
Ask it for a solution?

~ 303 ~

To live with integrity means ...

~ 304 ~

Suffering means …

~ 305 ~

I am at my wits' end …

~ 306 ~

My favorite song is … Write about the memory you
associate with this song.

~ 307 ~

Dear _____, It's important to me that you know ...

~ 308 ~

How can I be content right now?

~ 309 ~

What words or dictums did you hear as a child that attacked
your self-esteem? Make a list and then challenge each of them
with the knowledge you have today.

~ 310 ~

Today I want …

~ 311 ~

I don't like anyone telling me that I can't …

~ 312 ~

I feel at my best when …

~ 313 ~

My relationship with money ... Explore whose
values or issues you carry regarding money.

~ 314 ~

I am in awe of ... Why?

~ 315 ~

Use all of your senses (sight, hearing, taste, touch, smell)
to describe your current state of mind.

~ 316 ~

It is difficult for me to accept … Why?

~ 317 ~

My best memory around food …

~ 318 ~

Regarding my religious heritage, I feel …

~ 319 ~

Go back to your journal writing from 7 days ago. Read what you wrote. What feeling does it evoke for you? Why?

~ 320 ~

Who are you in conflict with right now? Write him/her a letter and share how you feel. Write only from your own perspective and refrain from accusations.

~ 321 ~

The happiest day of my life ...

~ 322 ~

Today my body wants to tell me ...

~ 323 ~

I can be a better partner by ...

~ 324 ~

I feel sorry for ... Why?

~ 325 ~

How can I practice compassion at work or school?

~ 326 ~

I feel lack in my life when ...
I feel abundance in my life when ...

~ 327 ~

If I had more leisure time, I would ...
Why? I could begin to include this in my life by ...

~ 328 ~

Just for today …

~ 329 ~

How can I allow myself to relax and just "be"?
How can I implement this into my life?

~ 330 ~

How am I over committing to everyone but myself?
What can I do to balance this out?

~ 331 ~

What I love about myself is …

~ 332 ~

The difference between being alone and lonely is …

~ 333 ~

I can bring the fullness of who I am to my work life by …

~ 334 ~

When I have pain in my life, or make a mistake, instead of responding with self-incriminations, I can be loving and kind to myself by ...

~ 335 ~

For me to be "authentic" means ...

~ 336 ~

I love the feel of ... Describe and explore why.

~ 337 ~

The "Big Questions" in my life are ... Explore why.

~ 338 ~

I never have time to _____ anymore. (List 10 things)
Of those 10, which one most nourishes to you? Why?
Brainstorm ways you can bring it back into your life.

~ 339 ~

Use all of your senses (sight, hearing, taste, touch, smell)
to describe your greatest fear.

~ 340 ~

How can I create structure/organization in my life
that will help me to love and respect myself?

~ 341 ~

I feel expansive and creative when …

~ 342 ~

I never want to …

~ 343 ~

Consider all the roles you play in life ~ parent, sibling, friend, worker, etc. ~ in which role are you most comfortable? Explore why.

~ 344 ~

Sometimes I am angry at my body because ...

~ 345 ~

I feel guilty when I ... Explore why.

~ 346 ~

The most foolish thing I have ever done ...
Why was it foolish?

~ 347 ~

Right now I am most proud of ...

~ 348 ~

I am completely committed to ...

~ 349 ~

What small occurrence in your life has made
a big impact on you? Explore how and why.

~ 350 ~

Write a letter to someone and share all the reasons
you love him/her.

~ 351 ~

I want to be at peace with …

~ 352 ~

I have no faith in … Why?

~ 353 ~

The best adventure I've had …

~ 354 ~

I shut down when … Explore how and why.

~ 355 ~

There is too much …in my life. Why?

~ 356 ~

The most beautiful sound in the world …

~ 357 ~

Close your eyes. Consider the last 24 hours.
What moment or event stands out? Why?
Explore the emotion attached to this.

~ 358 ~

I will forever be connected to … Explore how and why.

~ 359 ~

When have you been a warrior and taken a stand.
Who or what were you fighting for? How and why?

~ 360 ~

There is not enough … in my life. Why?
How can you remedy this?

~ 361 ~

What does it mean to be gentle?

~ 362 ~

I express my creativity in my everyday life ...

~ 363 ~

To give or receive respect means ...

~ 364 ~

A year from now, I want …

~ 365 ~

Write a love letter to your Self.

May all you have discovered in your own words bring you greater understanding and deeper love & compassion for your Self and Others.

Prompt Index

Note: Other than the Letters, Lists and Dialogue categories, which index journaling techniques, the rest are theme related and offer the opportunity to write with focused intention on a particular subject. Many of the prompts overlap from category to category because heightening awareness of how these seemingly disparate areas of life (i.e. spiritual and career, or inward and health) actually affect one another is part of discovering ways to create a balanced, healthy life.

Letters:
21, 28, 74, 107, 151, 158, 165, 184, 194, 200, 228, 259, 287, 307, 320, 350, 365

Lists:
15, 31, 50, 68, 75, 90, 108, 119, 124, 132, 133, 159, 173, 176, 208, 218, 223, 229, 240, 251, 262, 273, 309, 338

Dialogue:
116, 149, 213, 231, 241

Inward Reflections:
3, 7, 11.14, 15, 17, 19, 21, 22, 24, 25, 26, 27, 30, 31, 33, 43, 36, 37, 38, 39, 40, 41, 42, 43, 44, 45, 47, 48, 50, 51, 52, 54, 55, 56, 57, 58, 59, 61, 62, 63, 64, 65, 66, 67, 68, 69, 70, 72, 73, 75, 76, 77, 78, 79, 80, 82, 83, 84, 85, 86, 88, 89, 90, 91, 92, 93, 94, 95, 96, 97, 98, 100, 102, 103, 104, 105, 106, 107, 108, 109, 111, 112, 113, 114, 115, 116, 118, 119, 120, 121, 122, 124, 125, 129, 130, 131, 132, 133, 136, 137, 138, 140, 1141, 142, 143, 145, 146, 148, 149, 152, 154, 156, 159, 160, 161, 162, 163, 164, 166, 168, 169, 170, 171, 172, 173, 174, 177, 179, 180, 182, 185, 187, 188, 191, 195, 196, 200, 202, 203, 205, 206, 207, 208, 209, 210, 211, 213, 217, 219, 221, 223, 226, 227, 229, 231, 234, 236, 237, 238, 239, 240, 242, 243, 244, 245, 246, 247, 248, 249, 250, 252, 253, 255, 256, 257,

258, 259, 260, 261, 262, 263, 264, 265, 266, 267, 268, 269, 270,
272, 273, 274, 275, 277, 279, 280, 282, 285, 286, 288, 289, 290,
291, 292, 293, 294, 295, 296, 297, 298, 299, 300, 301, 302, 303,
304, 308, 309, 310, 312, 314, 315, 316, 320, 322, 326, 328, 329,
331, 332, 333, 334, 335, 337, 338, 339, 340, 341, 342, 343, 344,
345, 347, 349, 351, 352, 354, 355, 356, 357, 358, 360, 361, 365

Outward Awareness:
10, 17, 19, 26, 28, 30, 33, 34, 35, 37, 38, 39, 41, 42, 43, 45, 46, 47,
48, 49, 50, 51, 52, 53, 55, 57, 58, 59, 60, 61, 62, 63, 64, 65, 66, 68,
69, 70, 71, 72, 74, 77, 78, 79, 81, 82, 84, 85, 86, 87, 88, 91, 92, 94,
95, 96, 97, 98, 99, 100, 101, 103, 105, 106, 108, 109, 110, 111,
114, 117, 119, 121, 122, 123, 124, 126, 127, 128, 129, 130, 131,
132, 133, 134, 135, 138, 139, 140, 141, 142, 144, 146, 147, 150,
151, 153, 156, 157, 158, 161, 163, 165, 166, 167, 168, 169, 172,
174, 175, 177, 178, 179, 181, 183, 189, 190, 192, 193, 194, 195,
196, 197, 199, 201, 202, 205, 206, 209, 210, 211, 212, 21, 216,
217, 218, 220, 222, 224, 225, 226, 227, 228, 230, 232, 233, 234,
235, 236, 237, 238, 239, 240, 241, 242, 244, 245, 247, 249, 251,
252, 254, 255, 256, 257, 258, 260, 261, 264, 265, 266, 268, 269,
271, 272, 274, 276, 278, 279, 280, 281, 283, 284, 287, 289, 291,
2932, 294, 296, 297, 299, 300, 301, 302, 303, 304, 305, 306, 307,
308, 310, 311, 312, 313, 314, 316, 317, 318, 820, 321, 323, 324,
325, 326, 327, 328, 329, 330, 333, 336, 338, 340, 343, 346, 347,
348, 349, 350, 351, 352, 353, 354, 355, 356, 357, 358, 359, 360,
361, 362, 363, 364

Awareness of Others:
19, 28, 33, 38, 39, 40, 41, 43, 46, 48, 49, 53, 55, 58, 59, 60, 61, 64,
66, 69, 72, 74, 78, 85, 92, 95, 98, 110, 111, 117, 122, 123, 124,
126, 128, 129, 131, 135, 138, 144, 147, 151, 157, 158, 163, 165,
167, 168, 169, 175, 182, 183, 189, 193, 194, 196, 197, 199, 206,
209, 210, 212, 216, 218, 220, 227, 228, 236, 238, 241, 242, 244,
247, 254, 255, 260, 261, 271, 272, 274, 276, 278, 281, 284, 286,
287, 289, 307, 310, 311, 320, 323, 324, 325, 330, 350, 351, 354,
358, 359, 363

Family Awareness:

8, 25, 28, 33, 38, 39, 40, 41, 43, 46, 47, 48, 49, 50, 51, 53, 55, 57, 58, 59, 60, 61, 62, 64, 65, 66, 70, 72, 78, 81, 82, 85, 91, 92, 95, 98, 104, 107, 110, 111, 113, 114, 115, 122, 123, 124, 126, 127, 129, 133, 134, 135, 138, 139, 146, 151, 157, 160, 163, 165, 167, 169, 170, 175, 182, 183, 189, 192, 193, 196, 206, 209, 210, 212, 219, 220, 226, 227, 228, 236, 238, 241, 242, 245, 247, 254, 255, 258, 260, 261, 268, 269, 271, 272, 274, 276, 277, 278, 279, 281, 282, 284, 285, 286, 287, 289, 292, 302, 305, 307, 308, 309, 310, 311, 316, 317, 318, 320, 323, 325, 328, 330, 343, 347, 348, 350, 351, 354, 363, 364

Spiritual Awareness:

3, 14, 19, 22, 23, 24, 31, 34, 36, 37, 38, 39, 40, 43, 44, 45, 47, 48, 49, 50, 51, 54, 55, 56, 57, 58, 61, 63, 64, 67, 70, 73, 75, 76, 78, 79, 80, 81, 83, 84, 85, 89, 90, 92, 93, 102, 104, 105, 107, 108, 112, 113, 117, 118, 121, 122, 124, 125, 126, 127, 130, 131, 134, 135, 136, 137, 138, 140, 141, 142, 143, 146, 148, 152, 154, 155, 159, 163, 171, 177, 186, 191, 200, 204, 206, 220, 221, 223, 226, 227, 230, 231, 234, 236, 238, 240, 242, 243, 246, 247, 248, 252, 257, 258, 259, 260, 261, 263, 265, 267, 269, 270, 271, 275, 277, 279, 282, 283, 286, 289, 290, 293, 295, 298, 299, 300, 304, 308, 310, 312, 318, 326, 328, 329, 332, 334, 337, 339, 341, 348, 351, 352, 356, 359, 360, 364, 365

Health Awareness:

19, 20, 21, 23, 25, 31, 32, 38, 39, 40, 42, 43, 45, 47, 48, 49, 50, 51, 52, 53, 54, 57, 58, 59, 61, 63, 65, 66, 67, 69, 70, 72, 76, 77, 78, 79, 81, 85, 87, 88, 91, 92, 95, 101, 103, 104, 105, 106, 107, 108, 109, 110, 111, 112, 113, 114, 116, 117, 119, 122, 124, 126, 129, 130, 131, 134, 136, 138, 139, 141, 142, 143, 146, 148, 156, 159, 163, 164, 166, 169, 173, 176, 187, 180, 181, 182, 184, 185, 188, 196, 198, 200, 201, 202, 210, 212, 213, 214, 223, 225, 226, 231, 232, 236, 237, 239, 242, 243, 245, 247, 253, 255, 259, 260, 261, 265, 266, 268, 271, 272, 273, 275, 277, 278, 279, 280, 282, 283, 289,

291, 295, 298, 302, 304, 305, 308, 309, 310, 312, 316, 317, 321,
322, 327, 328, 329, 330, 331, 334, 338, 340, 343, 344, 345, 347,
348, 351, 354, 360, 364, 365

Creative Awareness:
17, 23, 24, 25, 31, 32, 35, 36, 37, 38, 40, 43, 44, 45, 46, 47, 48, 49,
50, 51, 52, 53, 54, 56, 57, 58, 67, 69, 72, 74, 76, 81, 84, 85, 87, 90,
93, 95, 103, 104, 106, 112, 113, 116, 120, 121, 129, 130, 132, 134,
136, 138, 142, 154, 156, 181, 185, 191, 197, 200, 221, 226, 230,
234, 242, 244, 248, 257, 263, 293, 306, 310, 341, 362

Career (or School) Awareness:
16, 17, 30, 31, 32, 33, 35, 36, 38, 39, 40, 41, 43, 45, 47, 48, 49, 50,
51, 52, 53, 54, 57, 58. 59, 60, 61, 63, 64, 65, 66, 67, 68, 69, 70, 72,
73, 74, 75, 76, 77, 78, 79, 81, 84, 85, 86, 87, 88, 90, 91, 92, 93, 94,
95, 98, 100, 101, 103, 104, 106, 108, 109, 110, 111, 112, 113, 114,
115, 116, 117, 119, 120, 121, 122, 123, 124, 126, 128, 129, 130,
131, 132, 133, 134, 135, 136, 138, 139, 140, 141, 142, 143, 145,
146, 147, 148, 149, 151, 155, 156, 157, 158, 159, 162, 163, 164,
166, 167, 168, 169, 171, 172, 173, 174, 175, 176, 177, 179, 180,
181, 182, 183, 185, 187, 188, 189, 191, 193, 194, 195, 196, 197,
198, 200, 201, 202, 203, 204, 205, 206, 207, 208, 210, 211, 212,
213, 215, 217, 218, 219, 220, 222, 223, 225, 226, 227, 228, 229,
230, 231, 232, 233, 235, 236, 237, 238, 240, 242m 243, 245, 247,
248, 249, 250, 251, 252, 254, 255, 256, 258, 259, 260, 261, 262,
264, 265, 266, 267, 268, 269, 270, 271, 272, 273, 274, 275, 276,
277, 278, 279, 280, 281, 282, 283, 284, 288, 289, 292, 293, 295,
297, 298, 299, 300, 302, 303, 304, 305, 307, 308, 310, 311, 312,
313, 315, 316, 319, 320, 321, 323, 324, 325, 326, 327, 328, 329,
330, 331, 333, 334, 337, 338, 339, 340, 341, 342, 343, 345, 346,
347, 348, 349, 351, 352, 354, 355, 357, 359, 360, 363, 364, 365

References

1. Pennebaker, James W., Danna Graybeal, and Janel D. Sexton. "The Role of Story-Making in Disclosure Writing: The Psychometrics of Narrative." Psychology and Health 2002: Vol. 17, No. 5, pp. 571-581.

2. Pennebaker, James W. "Writing About Emotional Experiences As A Therapeutic Process." American Psychological Society May 1997: Vol. 8, No. 3.

3. Cameron, Julia, *The Artist's Way: A Spiritual Path to Higher Creativity* (New York: Penguin Putnam, 1992), p. 10, 12

4. Nelson, G. Lynn, *Writing and Being: Taking Back Our Lives Through the Power of Language* (Philadelphia: Innisfree, 1994), p. 37. 43, 44

5. Metcalf, Linda Trichter and Tobin Simon, *Writing the Mind Alive: The Proprioceptive Method for Finding Your Authentic Voice* (New York: Ballantine, 2002), Intro-xxi

Bibliography

These are some of the books that have been instrumental on my personal journey of writing for self-awareness:

Cameron, Julia. The Artist's Way: A Spiritual Path to Higher
Creativity. New York: Penguin Putnam, 1992.

Cameron, Julia. The Vein of Gold: A Journey to Your Creative
Heart. New York:
Penguin Putnam. 1996.

Capacchione, Lucia. The Creative Journal: The Art of Finding
Yourself. Athens: Ohio University P, 1979.

Csikszentmihalyi, Mihaly. Creativity: Flow and the Psychology of
Discovery and Invention. New York: HarperCollins,
1996.

Glouberman, Dr. Dina. Life Choices, Life Changes. London:
Hodder, 1989.

Goldberg, Natalie. Writing Down the Bones: Freeing the Writer
Within. Boston: Shambhala, 1986.

Jennings, Maureen. The Map of Your Mind: Journeys into
Creative Expression. Toronto: McClelland & Stewart,
2001.

Louden, Jennifer. The Woman's Retreat Book: A Guide to
Restoring, Rediscovering, and Reawakening Your True

Self – in a Moment, an Hour, a Day, or a Weekend. San Francisco: HarperCollins, 1997.

Matson, Clive. Let the Crazy Child Write: Finding Your Creative Writing Voice. Novato: New World, 1998.

Metcalf, Linda Trichter, and Tobin Simon. Writing the Mind Alive: The Proprioceptive Method for Finding Your Authentic Voice. New York: Ballantine, 2002.

Metzger, Deena, Writing for Your Life: A Guide and Companion to the Inner Worlds, San Francisco: HarperCollins, 1992.

Nelson, G. Lynn. Writing and Being: Taking Back Our Lives Through the Power of Language. Philadelphia: Innisfree, 1994.

Ornstein, Robert. The Right Mind: Making Sense of the Hemispheres. Orlando: Harcourt, 1997.

Rico, Gabriele. Writing the Natural Way. New York: Jeremy P. Tarcher/Putnam, 2000.

Schneider, Pat. Writing Alone with Others. New York: Oxford University P, 2003.

Sher, Gail, The Intuitive Writer: Listening to Your Own Voice, New York: Penguin
Putnam, 2002.

About the Author:

Plynn Gutman has been journaling for over 25 years. She holds an MFA in Creative Writing, has a private practice as an Integrated Life Coach and Energy Practitioner, and is the owner and co-facilitator of Your Liminal Space, which offers self-awareness retreats around the world. She is the former Director of the Young Adult Writing Project (YAWP), an ASU English Department summer writing program for 8th through 12th Grade students, and has facilitated workshops on personal awareness through writing in the US, Canada and the UAE.

Plynn is a self-professed home chef, who loves cooking without recipes, and blogs about her culinary adventures at "Cooking with Mom." She currently resides in Mesa, Arizona with her husband Michael and two delightful cats, Francis and Lucius.

Other books by Plynn:

The Work of Her Hands: A Prairie Woman's Life in Remembrances and Recipes
My Son Dave (the Duck): A Story About Loving and Letting Go

Your Journal Companion: iOS app / Android app

43908257R00111

Made in the USA
Middletown, DE
22 May 2017